WICKED WISDOM

Princess Dumebi Grace

AuthorHouse™
1663 Liberty Drive
Bloomington, IN 47403
www.authorhouse.com
Phone: 1 (800) 839-8640

Published by AuthorHouse: 07/24/2015

ISBN: 978-1-5049-2110-7 (sc)
ISBN: 978-1-5049-2111-4 (e)

Print information available on the last page.

Any people depicted in stock imagery provided by Thinkstock are models,
and such images are being used for illustrative purposes only.
Certain stock imagery © Thinkstock.

This book is printed on acid-free paper.

Scripture quotations marked KJV are from the Holy Bible, King James Version (Authorized Version). First published
in 1611. Quoted from the KJV Classic Reference Bible, Copyright © 1983 by The Zondervan Corporation.

*T*he book is an inspirational journey with verses taken from the bible and the a simpler meaning or application of the passage. Affirmations to attain the recommendations of the bible verse.

From

_____

_____

_____

_____

_____

_____

_____

_____

_____

All thanks and glory to the Divine mind, the I AM and everyone who has encouraged me and taught me lessons on this plain called earth. I thank my family especially my Dad, my big brother Anthony, my sister Lydia and her husband, Mudi Akpocha for holding things down for me when I needed them most. I thank my biggest supporter, King Duru, who tells me I can always do better. I thank my friends Uche Ken, Bash Elliotte, April Quiana, Molly, for being there for me. I appreciate you all. My baby celynez for your patience and understanding with mummy. My maternal uncle, Prince Jude Nwoko for your care and support out here in the USA. My salute goes to my cousin, HRH Charles Anyasi, the King of Idumuje - unor Kingdom, for your support, brotherly advice and words of wisdom. I remember all what you say to me. Thanks to My lawyer Barr Victor Ogoli for taking care of things for me. My sincere appreciation goes to Erin Cohen my publishing consultant and the Authorhouse team for making this project come alive in all its beauty and splendor. You guys Rock! Thank you all for your prayers and good energy thoughts towards me. I feel it. I send that loving energy back to you all   . I pray your wishes be fulfilled. THANK YOU.

THOSE WHO FEEL OPPRESSED

On the occasion of (write a personal message)

_____

_____

_____

_____

_____

_____

_____

_____

_____

_____

_____

THE LITTLE PERFECT GIFT

To:

_____

_____

_____

_____

_____

_____

_____

_____

_____

_____

Other mini books in this series

* *Wisdom calls again*

* *Wisdom for riches*

* *What is wisdom for a woman*

* *Wisdom for children*

The righteous man wisely considereth the house of the wicked: but God overthroweth the wicked fortheir wickedness.

Pro 21:12

God will never allow a bad person to have power over you or anyone for long.

Affirmations: I am thankful that I am aware and I am free from all trickery of wicked people. I refuse to be bullied by fear. I'm surrounded by good.

You will be destroyed by that which you have taken by trickery, wayo or magomago.

Affirmations: I am kindness and genuine, I and my properties are therefore protected.

The robbery of the wicked shall destroy them; because they refuse to do judgment.

Pro 21:7

*But the wicked shall be
cut off from the earth,
and the transgressors shall
be rooted out of it.*

Pro 2:22

An high look, and a proud heart, and the plowing of the wicked, is sin.

Pro 21:4

Ego and pride are placed at the same level as committing wickedness and they are all sin.

Affirmation: I am happy and grateful that I am secure and enlightened.

Judgment day must surely come for the wicked.

Affirmations: I am grateful I walk in love and the wicked are cut off from my world.

The wicked is cursed and the just is blessed, it is as simple as black and white. Choose to be good.

Affirmations: I and my family are just and we surrounded by loving people, we are so blessed.

A wise person in the place of authority should never allow wickedness and the people who perpetrate evil should be punished.

Affirmations: I am wise and give discipline to myself and others whenever necessary. I am power and strength

A wise king scattereth the wicked, and bringeth the wheel over them.

Pro 20:26

The curse of the LORD is in the house of the wicked: but he blesseth the habitation of the just.

Pro 3:33

Enter not into the path of the wicked, and go not in the way of evil men.

Pro 4:14

A brother offended is harder to be won than a strong city: and their contentions are like the bars of a castle.

Pro 18:19

Do everything possible not to offend the people you care about and especially the ones that care about you.

Never allow your friends to become your enemies. (frienemies)

Affirmations: I understand, and I am understood by family and friends, love rules amongst us.

Do not join evil gangs, clubs or fraternities. It is wickedness to yourself and your family.

Affirmations: my steps lead me to good daily, my friendships and affiliations are with good people.

This world is a market place, you do not throws stones in the market. But the wicked is not so wise, they end up falling into their own trap unawares.

Affirmations: I am happy my decisions and actions are for the greater good of mankind

Beware of talebearers, aprokos and tatafos because they will cause trouble in your friendships, your office and your home.

Affirmations: I am surrounded by people who are secure and are peace lovers.

A froward man soweth strife: and a whisperer separateth chief friends.

Pro 16:28

The way of the wicked is as darkness: they know not at what they stumble.

Pro 4:19

Put away from thee a forward mouth, and perverse lips put far from thee.

Pro 4:24

*An ungodly man diggeth
up evil: and in his lips there
is as a burning fire.*

Pro 16:27

Any time a person who does not fear God speaks into a matter, his/her words are always for destruction like a raging wildfire.

Affirmations: I am positive, I am responsible with my speech for peaceful solutions.

Watch what you say. If you
must speak, speak in kindness,
love and with discretion.

Affirmations: my utterances and
the things I say are full of wisdom,
empathy and love always.

You say something mean about someone or to someone and you jokingly tell people around that you are just being naughty… no that is wickedness.

affirmations: The things I say and do will be to bless and uplift people.

I am kind.

If you are in a place of authority, it is an abomination to be wicked. People should not confuse wickedness with discipline.

Affirmations: I am a royal priesthood, I do good to people. I am established in doing right.

It is an abomination to kings to commit wickedness: for the throne is established by righteousness.

Pro 16:12

*A naughty person, a wicked man,
walketh with a froward mouth.*

Pro 6:12

These six things doth the LORD hate: yea, seven are an abomination unto him:

Pro 6:16

The LORD is far from the wicked: but he heareth the prayer of the righteous.

Pro 15:29

If you feel that your prayers are not being answered, cry unto God like king David, say: "search me oh Lord if their be any wicked ways in me and lead me in the right path".

If my people who are called by name, shall humble themselves and pray and turn from their wicked ways, I'll hear and I'll heal their land.

Affirmations: my heart is free from wickedness, I'm healed.

These are wicked acts and God hates them:

- A proud look
- A lying tongue
- A hand that sheds innocent blood
- An heart that devises wicked imaginations
- Feet that be swift to running to mischief
- A false witness that speaks lies

This is an abomination before God:

- He that sows discord among brethren

Affirmation: I am a divine and infinite being, I have no need of the low human ego. I am truth and life. My imaginations and actions are of pure love.
I will only be a witness to the truth if I have to say any thing at all. I have the mind of Christ.
(repeat)

A wise person answers with discretion and understanding but evil comes out of the wicked person's mouth without caution

The heart of the righteous studieth to answer: but the mouth of the wicked poureth out evil things.

Pro 15:28

My mission on earth is to be the advocate of peace, between man and God, between friends, between husband and wife, parents and children, between siblings and relatives, between men and women, between humans and nature. I am a peace maker. I live in divine order. (repeat)

Anyone quick to start a riot or destroy property is a mean person. Wickedness starts from your thoughts and the imaginations of what you will do when you get the opportunity. Consciously Stop evil thoughts.

Affirmations: I am quick and smart in doing good. My steps are ordered by God.

The thoughts of the wicked are an abomination to the LORD: but the words of the pure are pleasant words.

Pro 15:26

God searches the depth of your thoughts in everything you say or didn't say and in everything you do or didn't do, (Even when you ask for wealth) whether they are pure or they are wicked. God knows

Affirmations: my motives are not to oppress but for the greater good of humanity.

An heart that deviseth wicked imaginations, feet that be swift in running to mischief

Pro 6:18

He that reproveth a scorner getteth to himself shame: and he that rebuketh a wicked man getteth himself a blot.

Pro 9:7

When you are not upright in your ways, then you are wicked and your sacrifices and offering will be an abomination instead of a pleasure to God.

Affirmations: my heart is pure, I am light, I am loved by GOD.

The sacrifice of the wicked is an abomination to the LORD: but the prayer of the upright is his delight.

Pro 15:8

Do not bother to advice or correct a wicked person, he will start to plan evil against you. You can only pray for a wicked person.

I am grateful, I am surrounded by happy people with good intentions.

Doing good with wisdom and discretion will protect you from evil plans of wicked persons.
Affirmations:

Everything I do will lead to my own good, the good of the people around me and humanity in general.

The evil bow before the good; and the wicked at the gates of the righteous.

Pro 14:19

The good and the righteous will always have the most valuable, long lasting solution that is needed. Choose good and avoid evil so you can be the head.

Affirmations: I choose good, I choose to be happy, I choose to reign in victory.

Treasures of wickedness profit nothing: but righteousness delivereth from death.

Pro 10:2

The memory of the just is blessed: but the name of the wicked shall rot.

Pro 10:7

Nobody likes anyone who is always angry or scheming evil against people. Even the people planning evil with you, hate you. Don't be deceived.

Affirmations: I control my temper, I am honourable, and I am kind.

He that is soon angry dealeth foolishly: and a man of wicked devices is hated.

Pro 14:17

Eventually, all wickedness
will lead to rottenness.

Affirmations: I have the mark of Christ,
my name is blessed, anywhere my name is
mentioned will be for good and success.

If you see someone that is always talkingabout fighting, destroying things, destroying people with their mouth and what they say and if he or she can't get it, then no one else can get it, That person is a wicked person. Refuse to be influenced by such people.

Affirmations: I influence people with good and I am influenced by good and successful people.

The righteous eateth to the satisfying of his soul: but the belly of the wicked shall want.

Pro 13:25

The wicked is never satisfied.

If you are never satisfied with anything or anyone, watch yourself, wickedness is lurking in your heart.

Pray against it.

Affirmations I am grateful and happy, my needs are met daily and I have more than I could ever need, I am blessed.

The mouth of a righteous man is a well of life: but violence covereth the mouth of the wicked

Pro 10:11

The labour of the righteous
tendeth to life: the fruit
of the wicked to sin.

Pro 10:16

Out of the abundance of the heart, the mouth speaks. Whatever you say out of your mouth could be used against you.

Affirmations: I am happy and grateful God delivers me and my family daily from troubles and my speech is blessed.

The wicked is snared by the transgression of his lips: but the just shall come out of trouble.

Pro 12:13

Whatever a just man does will always lead to life. wickedness is sin and leads to death.

Affirmations: I am a just person in all my associations and my activities lead to happy living.

If you have been able to find out a wicked person, you should know that every action or word that comes out of him/her worth's almost nothing. Don't trust a wicked person.

Affirmations: I am surrounded by faithful and trustworthy people.

*He that withholdeth corn,
the people shall curse him:
but blessing shall be upon the
head of him that selleth it.*

Pro 11:26

Creating artificial scarcity of essential commodities and goods is wickedness, and wickedness is sin and the curses people send, will surely work.

Affirmations: I am blessed, I have the good interest of humanity at heart.

The tongue of the just is as choice silver: the heart of the wicked is little worth.

Pro 10:20

The fear of the wicked, it shall come upon him: but the desire of the righteous shall be granted.

Pro 10:24

If you enjoy planning evil actively or passively with others or know about the evil plan and you do nothing to stop it, you will also endure the punishment when karma comes calling and no one can deliver you.

Affirmations: I am protected by GOD, I participate only in good and amazing plans and activities

Though hand join in hand, the wicked shall not be unpun ished: but the seed of the righteous shall be delivered.

Pro 11:21

It pays to be good. A person becomes mean and wicked to people because of his or her insecurities and fears. More often than not, their fears catch up with them. They loose out eventually.

Affirmations: I am receiving answers to my prayers, my requests are granted.

Everything the wicked gathers to keep for his generations, quickly disappears and is squandered as soon as he or she dies. Wickedness is not profitable...wickedness no dey pay.

Affirmations: my foundation is eternal, my wealth is everlasting.

The merciful man doeth good to his own soul: but he that is cruel troubleth his own flesh.

Pro 11:17

When you forgive people who offend you, you protect yourself from sickness and you keep your soul happy.

It's been said that some sicknesses had been cured when the person forgives especially someone close; a spouse or a very close friend or sibling.

Affirmations: For my own good, I forgive the people who offend me and hold no grudge. I'm free.

As the whirlwind passeth, so is the wicked no more: but the righteous is an everlasting foundation.

Pro 10:25

The fear of the LORD prolongeth days: but the years of the wicked shall be shortened.

Pro 10:27

Whatever a man sows, he shall reap. A wicked plan always backfires.

Affirmations: my steps and actions are ordered by the wisdom of God and I find breakthroughs daily.

The righteousness of the perfect shall direct his way: but the wicked shall fall by his own wickedness.

Pro 11:5

To be wicked or to bear wicked thoughts (unforgiveness is wickedness) is the fastest way to die young.

Affirmations: I forgive and I bear no grudge against people, I am love.

A good person who follows God can never loose in this world.

Affirmations: I am a winner, I am positioned to be successful.

The righteous shall never be removed: but the wicked shall not inhabit the earth.

Pro 10:30

Write your notes

_____

_____

_____

_____

_____

_____

_____

_____

_____

_____

_____

Write your notes

_____

_____

_____

_____

_____

_____

_____

_____

_____

_____

_____

Write your notes

About the Author

Born in warri, Nigeria into the Royal Family (Idumu-Obi) from Idumuje - unor Kingdom, Delta State Nigeria. A happy mother to an amazing daughter, Princess Celynez, a sister to Princesses Lydia, Hope, Esther, Prince Anthony, Emmanuel and the daughter of the former Regent Prince Deacon D.I Echiemunor. Aunt to wonderful Nieces and Nephews. A multi- linguist, graduate of foreign Languages and Literatures from the University of Nigeria, Nsukka. Worked for over a Decade in the Nigerian Aviation Industry as Cabin Crew and Senior Cabin Crew member. An entertainer, event organizer and the CEO of Dumebigrace international limited (DGI Limited). Into Inspiration and spiritual journeys and a grateful Christian.